D1540462

Angel Blessings

A Touch of Love from Heaven Above

Paintings by

SANDRA KUCK

HARVEST HOUSE PUBLISHERS

EUGENE, OREGON

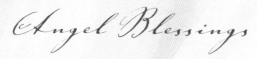

Angel Blessings

Copyright © 2003 by Harvest House Publishers
Eugene, Oregon 97402

ISBN 0-7369-1042-5

> V.F. Fine Arts, Inc.
> 1737 Stibbens St. #240B
> Houston, TX 77043
> 1.800.648.0405

Design and production by Garborg Design Works, Minneapolis, Minnesota

Printed in Hong Kong.

03 04 05 06 07 08 09 10 / NG / 8 7 6 5 4 3 2 1

Let no one ever
come to you
without leaving
better and happier.
Be the living
expression of God's
kindness: kindness
in your face,
kindness in your
eyes, kindness in
your smile.

MOTHER TERESA

3

Faith is always the channel of innumerable blessings.

CHARLES SPURGEON

*Too often we
underestimate the
power of a touch,
a smile, a kind word,
a listening ear,
an honest compliment,
or the smallest act of
caring, all of which
have the potential to
turn a life around.*

LEO BUSCAGLIA

BUT THE FRUIT OF THE

SPIRIT IS LOVE, JOY,

PEACE, PATIENCE,

KINDNESS, GOODNESS,

FAITHFULNESS, GENTLENESS

AND SELF-CONTROL.

AGAINST SUCH THINGS

THERE IS NO LAW.

THE BOOK OF GALATIANS

5

He who sows courtesy reaps
friendship, and he who
plants kindness gathers love.

SAINT BASIL

Kindness consists in
loving people more
than they deserve.

JACQUELINE SCHIFF

LITTLE DEEDS OF KINDNESS,
LITTLE WORDS OF LOVE,
MAKE OUR EARTH AN EDEN,
LIKE THE HEAVEN ABOVE.

JULIA A. CARNEY

A kiss without a hug is like a flower without the fragrance.

MALTESE PROVERB

A word of kindness is seldom spoken in vain, while witty sayings are as easily lost as the pearls slipping from a broken string.

GEORGE D. PRENTICE

We're "counting" the blessings, our joys we record,
The wonderful mercies like sunbeams outpoured;
But let us remember while praising the Lord,
Somebody else needs a blessing.

Somebody else needs a blessing,
Somebody else needs a blessing;
We'll let our lights shine to His glory divine,
Somebody else needs a blessing.

ELIZA HEWITT

CONSTANT KINDNESS CAN ACCOMPLISH MUCH. AS THE SUN
MAKES ICE MELT, KINDNESS CAUSES MISUNDERSTANDING,
MISTRUST, AND HOSTILITY TO EVAPORATE.

ALBERT SCHWEITZER

It's what each of us sows, and how, that gives to us character and prestige. Seeds of kindness, goodwill, and human understanding, planted in fertile soil, spring up into deathless friendships, big deeds of worth, and a memory that will not soon fade...

GEORGE MATTHEW ADAMS

The flower of kindness
will grow.
Maybe not now,
but it will some day.
And in kind that
kindness will flow,
For kindness grows
in this way.

ROBERT ALAN

Kindness is the language which the deaf can hear and the blind can see.

MARK TWAIN

Sandra Kuck
©2000

You cannot do a
kindness too soon,
for you never know
how soon it will be
too late.

RALPH WALDO
EMERSON

12

THROUGH THIS TOILSOME WORLD, ALAS!

ONCE AND ONLY ONCE I PASS;

IF A KINDNESS I MAY SHOW,

IF A GOOD DEED I MAY DO

TO A SUFFERING FELLOW MAN,

LET ME DO IT WHILE I CAN.

NO DELAY, FOR IT IS PLAIN

I SHALL NOT PASS THIS WAY AGAIN.

AUTHOR UNKNOWN

Kind words can be short and easy to speak,
but their echoes are truly endless.
MOTHER TERESA

HE THAT HAS DONE
YOU A KINDNESS WILL
BE MORE READY TO DO
YOU ANOTHER, THAN
HE WHOM YOU YOUR-
SELF HAVE OBLIGED.

BENJAMIN FRANKLIN

We cannot tell the precise
moment when friendship
is formed. As in filling a
vessel drop by drop, there
is at last a drop which
makes it run over. So in a
series of kindness there
is, at last, one which
makes the heart run over.

JAMES BOSWELL

For this very reason, make

every effort to add to your

faith goodness; and to

goodness, knowledge; and to

knowledge, self-control; and

to self-control, perseverance;

and to perseverance,

godliness; and to godliness,

brotherly kindness; and to

brotherly kindness, love.

THE BOOK OF 2 PETER

*You can't live a perfect day
without doing something
for someone who will never
be able to repay you.*

JOHN WOODEN

Never tire of loyalty and
kindness. Hold these virtues
tightly. Write them deep
within your heart.

THE BOOK OF PROVERBS (TLB)

IF SOMEONE LISTENS, OR
STRETCHES OUT A HAND,
OR WHISPERS A KIND
WORD OF ENCOURAGE-
MENT, OR ATTEMPTS TO
UNDERSTAND A LONELY
PERSON, EXTRAORDINARY
THINGS BEGIN TO HAPPEN.

LORETTA GIRZARTIS

*Great opportunities to help
others seldom come,
but small ones surround us daily.*

SALLY KOCH

Blessings crown the head of the righteous.

THE BOOK OF PROVERBS

18

Happiness comes from spiritual wealth, not material
wealth...Happiness comes from giving, not getting.
If we try hard to bring happiness to others, we cannot
stop it from coming to us also. To get joy, we must
give it, and to keep joy, we must scatter it.

JOHN TEMPLETON

If I can stop one heart from breaking,
I shall not live in vain;
If I can ease one life the aching,
Or cool one pain,
Or help one fainting robin
Up to his nest again,
I shall not live in vain.

EMILY DICKINSON

IT IS THE SWEET, SIMPLE THINGS OF LIFE
WHICH ARE THE REAL ONES AFTER ALL.

LAURA INGALLS WILDER

A lifelong blessing for children is to fill them with warm memories of times together. Happy memories become treasures in the heart to pull out on the tough days of adulthood.

CHARLOTTE KASL

KINDNESS MAKES THE DIFFERENCE BETWEEN PASSION AND CARING. KINDNESS IS TENDERNESS. KINDNESS IS LOVE, BUT PERHAPS GREATER THAN LOVE... KINDNESS IS GOOD WILL. KINDNESS SAYS, "I WANT YOU TO BE HAPPY." KINDNESS COMES VERY CLOSE TO THE BENEVOLENCE OF GOD.

RANDOLPH RAY

Lord, dismiss us with Thy blessing,
Hope, and comfort from above;
Let us each, Thy peace possessing,
Triumph in redeeming love.

AUTHOR UNKNOWN

Kindness, nobler ever than revenge.

WILLIAM SHAKESPEARE

The supreme happiness in life is

loved for ourselves, or rather,

Truth and kindness in sweet embrace,
Righteousness and peace are God's grace;
For truth out of the earth does spring,
And righteousness from heaven ring.

FAYE T. BRESLER

THE HAPPIEST HEART THAT EVER BEAT

WAS IN SOME QUIET BREAST

THAT FOUND THE COMMON DAYLIGHT SWEET,

AND LEFT TO HEAVEN THE REST.

JOHN V. CHENEY

the conviction that we are loved—

loved in spite of ourselves.

VICTOR HUGO

"Then the King will say to those on his right, 'Come, you who are blessed by my Father; take your inheritance, the kingdom prepared for you since the creation of the world. For I was hungry and you gave me something to eat, I was thirsty and you gave me something to drink, I was a stranger and you invited me in, I needed clothes and you clothed me, I was sick and you looked after me, I was in prison and you came to visit me.'

"Then the righteous will answer him, 'Lord, when did we see you hungry and feed you, or thirsty and give you something to drink? When did we see you a stranger and invite you in, or needing clothes and clothe you? When did we see you sick or in prison and go to visit you?'

"The King will reply, 'I tell you the truth, whatever you did for one of the least of these brothers of mine, you did for me.'"

THE BOOK OF MATTHEW

Do unto others as you would have them do unto you.
THE GOLDEN RULE

Be not forgetful to entertain strangers:
for thereby some have entertained angels unawares.

THE BOOK OF HEBREWS (KJV)

A kind heart is a
fountain of gladness,
making everything in
its vicinity freshen
into smiles.

WASHINGTON IRVING

There shall be showers of blessing,
If we but trust and obey;
There shall be seasons refreshing,
If we let God have His way.

Showers of blessing,
Showers of blessing we need:
Mercy drops round us are falling,
But for the showers we plead.

DANIEL WHITTLE

ONE WHO KNOWS

HOW TO SHOW

AND TO ACCEPT

KINDNESS WILL BE A

FRIEND BETTER THAN

ANY POSSESSION.

SOPHOCLES

Whatever you do,
do it with kindness and love.

THE BOOK OF 2 CORINTHIANS (TLB)

Fair and softly goes far.

MIGUEL DE CERVANTES

It is futile to judge a kind deed by its motives.
Kindness can become its own motive. We are
made kind by being kind.

ERIC HOFFER

If you were busy being kind,
Before you knew it, you would find
You'd soon forget to think 'twas true
That someone was unkind to you.
If you were busy being glad,
And cheering people who are sad,
Although your heart might ache a bit,
You'd soon forget to notice it.

R. FOREMAN

So, amid the conflict whether great or small,
Do not be disheartened, God is over all;
Count your many blessings, angels will attend,
Help and comfort give you to your journey's end.

JOHNSON OATMAN, JR.

DO ALL THE GOOD YOU CAN. BY ALL THE MEANS YOU CAN. IN ALL THE WAYS YOU CAN. IN ALL THE PLACES YOU CAN. AT ALL THE TIMES YOU CAN. TO ALL THE PEOPLE YOU CAN. AS LONG AS EVER YOU CAN.

JOHN WESLEY

The words of kindness are more healing to a drooping heart than balm or honey.

SARAH FIELDING

Have you had a kindness shown?
Pass it on; 'twas not given for thee alone,
Pass it on; Let it travel down the years,
Let it wipe another's tears,
Till in heaven the deed appears,
Pass it on.

HENRY BURTON

To cultivate kindness is a valuable part of the business of life.

SAMUEL JOHNSON

Therefore, as God's
chosen people, holy
and dearly loved,
clothe yourselves with
compassion, kindness,
humility, gentleness
and patience. Bear
with each other and
forgive whatever
grievances you may
have against one
another. Forgive as the
Lord forgave you.

THE BOOK OF
COLOSSIANS